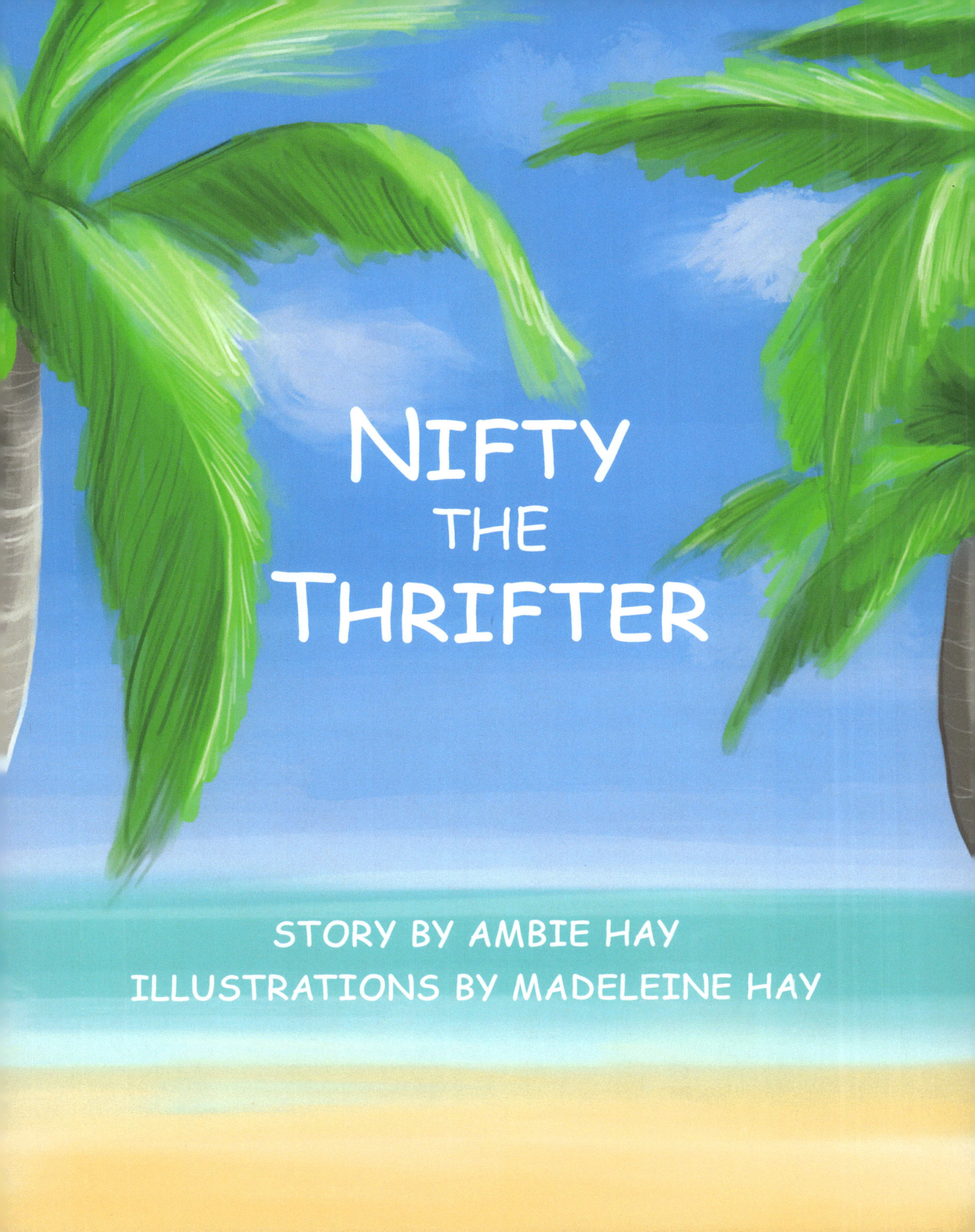

Copyright © Ambie Hay and Madeleine Hay 2021
Story and Writing by Ambie Hay
Illustrations, Graphics, & Layout by Madeleine Hay

ISBN 978-0-578-84170-0

To learn more about Nifty, visit:
www.niftythethrifter.com
and
www.thepalmbeachthrifters.com

This book is dedicated to all the cheerful thrift shop volunteers and to all those who generously donate.

In a sunny little town between the palm trees and the sea,

lives Nifty the Thrifter!

Thrifting is fun. You never know what you'll find. There is always a surprise around every corner.

You can be a thrift shopper too!

Off we go!
"Let's be thrifty," says Nifty!

# Reasons Why Nifty Loves Thrifting

## GIVING BACK
With every purchase you make at a thrift shop the money goes towards a charity. It gives you a warm heart.

## SAVE MONEY
Everyone loves saving money and getting great deals.

He stacks stuff on shelves.

He carries out boxes.

And he greets customers at the door with a sparkly smile!

Off we go!
"Let's be thrifty," says Nifty!

Sew it    Paint it    Glue it    Frame it!

You can decorate your room, too. And don't forget to be sparkly!

Off we go!
"Let's be thrifty," says Nifty!

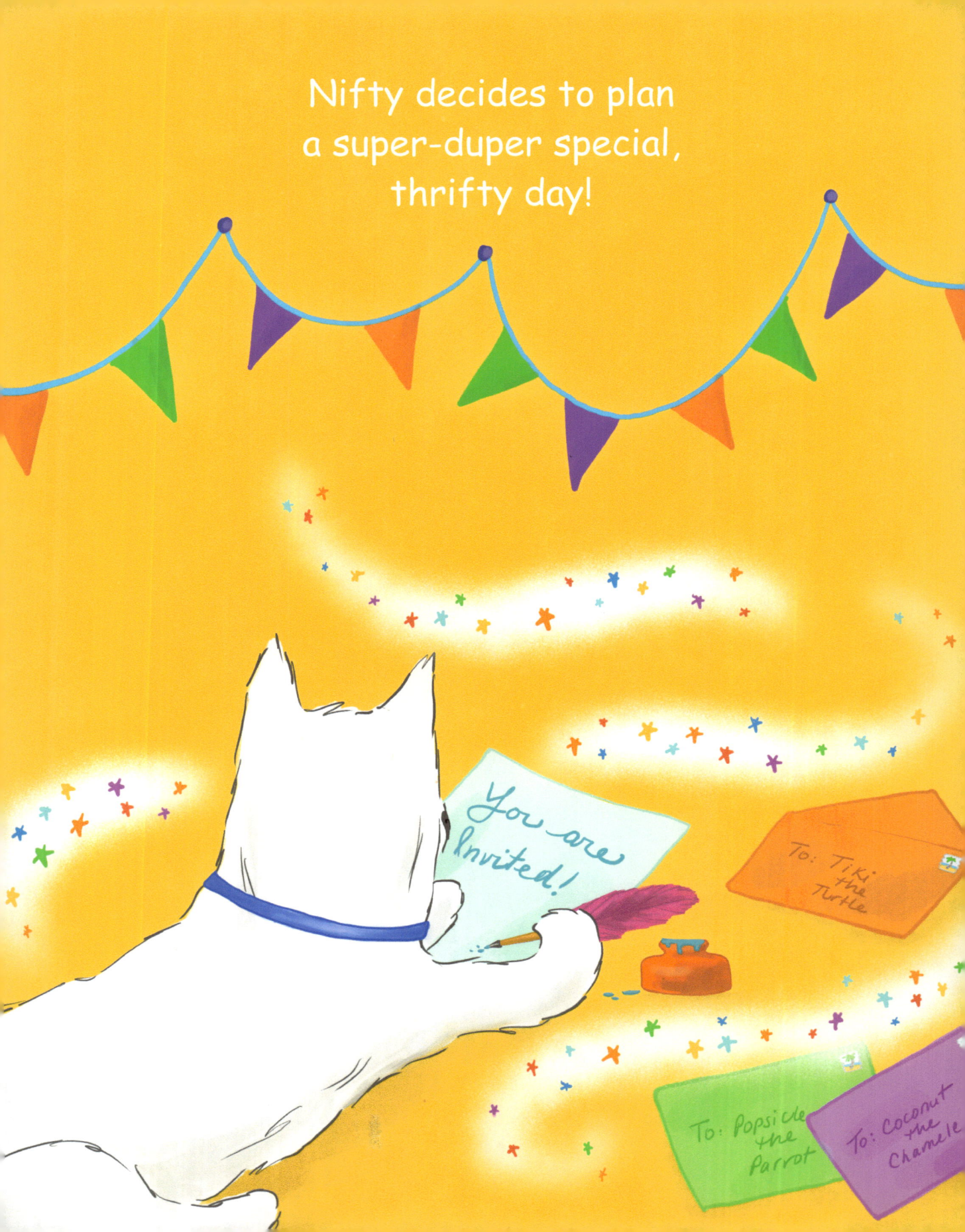

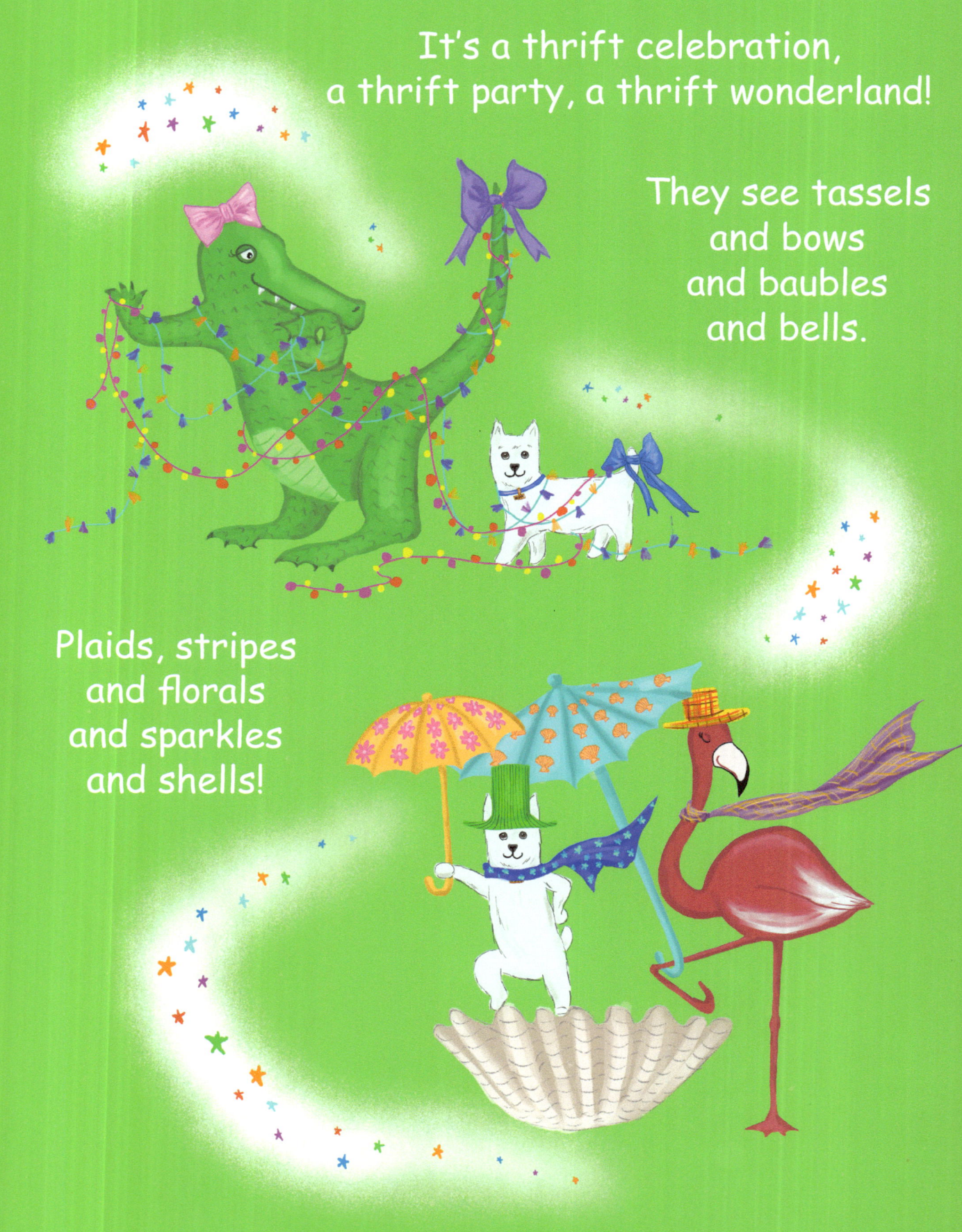

It's a thrift celebration,
a thrift party, a thrift wonderland!

They see tassels
and bows
and baubles
and bells.

Plaids, stripes
and florals
and sparkles
and shells!

Mountains of books,

and mirrors and things.

Antique tables, settees

and butterfly wings!

## ABOUT THE AUTHOR

Ambie Hay is a thrifter, writer, and artist.
Ambie goes on daily thrifting adventures with her furry
friend, Sailor who inspired this book. Living in Florida
she enjoys the sunshine, and her work is inspired
by the never-ending beauty of nature
and the tropical shores.

## ABOUT THE ILLUSTRATOR

Madeleine Hay is an artist and designer who
lives between the seaside coast of New England
and the blugegrass meadows of the Midwest.
She graduated from RISD and now finds endless
inspiration making art and weaving magic
into all of her creations.

CPSIA information can be obtained
at www.ICGtesting.com
Printed in the USA
LVHW071028100621
688624LV00016B/53